PENGUIN BOOKS

HOW TO BE DECADENT

George Mikes was born in 1912 in Siklós, Hungary. He studied law and received his doctorate at Budapest University. At the same time he became a journalist and was sent to London as a correspondent to cover the Munich crisis. He came for a fortnight and has stayed ever since. During the war he was engaged in broadcasting to Hungary and at the time of the Revolution he went back to cover that event for B.B.C. television.

Mr Mikes now works as a critic, broadcaster and writer. His books include *The Hungarian Revolution*, *Über Alles*, *Little Cabbages*, *Shakespeare and Myself*, *Italy for Beginners*, *How to Unite Nations*, *How to be an Alien*, *How to be Inimitable*, *How to Scrape Skies*, *How to Tango* and *How to Run a Stately Home* (with the Duke of Bedford). He has also published a novel, *Mortal Passion*. His latest publications are *George Mikes Introduces Switzerland* (1977; edited by Raffael Ganz) and *Tsi-Tsa* (1978). Many of his books have been published in Penguin. Mr Mikes is married with two children and enjoys getting away from the countryside.

Nicolas Bentley was born in Highgate in 1907 and educated at University College School, London, and Heatherley School of Art. He was an artist, author, publisher and illustrator of more than sixty books – including works by Belloc, T. S. Eliot, Damon Runyon and Lawrence Durrell, as well as several other books with George Mikes. He died in 1978.

BLACK
DWARF

NICOZAS
BENTLEY

GEORGE MIKES

How to be Decadent

Nicolas Bentley drew the pictures

PENGUIN BOOKS

Penguin Books Ltd, Harmondsworth, Middlesex, England
Penguin Books, 625 Madison Avenue, New York, New York 10022, U.S.A.
Penguin Books Australia Ltd, Ringwood, Victoria, Australia
Penguin Books Canada Ltd, 2801 John Street, Markham, Ontario, Canada L3R 1B4
Penguin Books (N.Z.) Ltd, 182-190 Wairau Road, Auckland 10, New Zealand

———

First published by André Deutsch 1977
Published in Penguin Books 1981

———

Copyright © George Mikes, 1977
All rights reserved

———

Reproduced, printed and bound in Great Britain by
Cox and Wyman Ltd, Reading
Set in Linotype Georgian

To my dear old friend, Emeric Pressburger –
the only man I know who is not decadent.
But – I hope – he can learn.

Contents

For Some Time There'll be an England . . .   *page* 9

On the Elegance of Decay   11

Old and New   16

Language   20

Food   23

Drinks   29

Shopping   32

Sex   36

On Cat-Worship   40

On How Not to be Reserved   45

On the National Passion   47

On Not Complaining   51

Bank Holidays   53

Buses   56

How to Get Lost in London   57

How to Panic Quietly   60

On Fiddling Through   65

The Generation Gap   67

Is the Economy Really on the Mend?   69

How to Lose an Empire   72

How to Become a Colony   79

On Ceasing to be an Island   83

Envoi   85

'But you are ruining the country!'

For Some Time
There'll be an England . . .

THESE are great years for the British. The nation has not been so gloriously united since the days of Churchill, but a blind and unappreciative world fails to see the light.

Some time ago a businessman friend of mine remarked about a Trotskyist Trade Union faction which was holding up the settlement of a damaging strike by insisting on some ludicrous and impossible demands: 'They are incredibly stupid. Don't they see that they are ruining the country?' But as their aim *was* to ruin the country they were not stupid, whatever else they may have been.

Similarly, the world fails to understand the British and appreciate what they are doing. The British – as the whole world, particularly the British themselves, keep saying – are the most fair-minded people in the world. After the Second World War they declared: 'Let's be fair. We have been Top Nation for centuries. We have done splendidly well once again. Now we must give others a chance. Let's decline.'

But it is not so easy to decline as the uninitiated imagine. After a few centuries other nations just will not believe that you are as inefficient and couldn't-care-less as you are. They will insist on thinking of you as

9

successful, reliable and rich, however unsuccessful, un-
reliable and poor you may have become. Declining needs
the effort of a united nation – not just one class, one
layer; not just the politicians. It needs the unfailing
effort of rich and poor, old and young, intellectual and
illiterate, skilled and unskilled, shop floor and manage-
ment. It is an arduous, almost herculean task but nothing
will deter the British, once they have made up their
minds. They played a great part in destroying Nazi
Germany; the destruction of democratic Britain seems
child's play compared with that.

The general strategy was grandiose: let us give away
our Empire as fast as possible or a little faster; let us
ruin the pound sterling by pretending that we did not
give away our Empire and can still be a reserve currency;
let us ruin the City and then rely on it as our main source
of strength; let us distribute overseas aid in a grand
manner, at the same time, let us go around begging, cap
in hand; *Made in Britain* used to be synonymous with
superlative quality, so let us not rest until it means
'shoddy goods, delivered late'; and let us divide the
country into small sections. If Cyprus can be independent,
why not Wales? If Malta, why not Lancashire or Corn-
wall? If Singapore, why not Birmingham? If Field
Marshal Idi Amin can make a fool of himself – well,
didn't he learn everything from us?

All this needed great determination, skill and the
united effort of a great nation. But the British aren't the
British for nothing. To their eternal glory, they are on
the way to complete success.

On the Elegance of Decay

IT was not only that proverbial spirit of fairness that led the nation to this decision. There was another, equally good reason. To remain Top Nation would inevitably have meant *winning* the eternal rat-race from time to time – perhaps quite often – and that the British cannot bear. The thing is to take part but not to win. You take part only and exclusively because without taking part *you cannot lose*. This is not the Nation of Vulgar Winners; this is the Nation of Good Losers.

The greatest days of Rome were its days of decline. The most splendid period of the Bourbon monarchy was the period before the Revolution. It is more elegant, wise and stylish to decay than to flourish; better to decline than to pant, rush around, sweat and get hoarse in vulgar bargaining. It is much more in keeping with the British style to live in a quiet and slightly disintegrating manor house than in a super-modern and noisy market place. It is more in keeping to potter around in the garden and remain healthy than to rush around town under great stress and get heart attacks. I agree with the British about this; I too prefer constructive decay to futile progress. But one has to *know* how to decay; one must learn how to be decadent. You may desire to decay, yet your inborn excellence, your splendid human qualities, your shining character may keep you on the top. Or else, you may overdo it and decay a shade too speedily.

*   *   *

Once upon a time I committed another little book, called *How to be an Alien*. A good friend, to my horror, discovered in 1976 that that book was thirty years old. I have reluctantly to admit that although I was only four years old when I wrote it, this makes me almost middle-aged.

What has changed in thirty years? *Who* has changed in thirty years? Would I write that book again? *Could* I write that book again? If I did try to write it, in what way would it differ from the original *How to be an Alien*?

Both I and Britain have, of course, changed a great deal. First of all, I have become, in a sense, more British than the British while the British have become less British. I have become a little better off than the young refugee was thirty years ago, Britain has become much poorer. I have climbed up the ladder a bit, Britain has climbed down quite a lot. I have become less of a European, Britain – apparently – more European. Britain has lost an Empire and gained me (the net gain, let's face it, is infinitesimal).

How to be an Alien was addressed to fellow aliens, telling them how to make themselves acceptable, how to imitate the English – in other, simple words *How to be an Alien* was telling them how not to be an Alien.

There was a joke at the end of the forties. A German refugee was offered naturalisation but he indignantly

Ups and downs

exclaimed: 'What? Without India?!' He had a point, of course. But should you still wish to belong to the clan – India or no India – you must go through a refresher course if you are an ancient alien like myself, or learn some new rules if you are a newcomer, a budding alien. You still have to discuss the weather, of course, with fervent interest; you still have to form an orderly queue on the slightest provocation; you are still not to address a shop-assistant until you are spoken to; if you are a worker, you are not to work, if you are a solicitor you are not to solicit, if you are a streetwalker you are not to walk the streets, if you are the Lord Privy Seal you are not a lord and if you are the Black Rod you most certainly are not black (nor, for that matter, are you a rod). But English ideas on food, drink, sex, travel etc have changed or been modified, so study the new rules carefully.

The most important thing to remain unchanged is the English attitude towards you. The world still consists of two clearly divided groups: the English and the foreigners. One group consists of less than fifty million people; the other of 3,950 million. The latter group does not really count. The Scots, the Welsh, the Irish and – more or less – the Australians and the Americans are neither English nor foreigners: they are the Scots, the Welsh, the Irish, the Australians and the Americans, but they are as ludicrous as foreigners. Bloody foreigners are rarely called bloody foreigners nowadays, some say because the English have become more polite; my own feeling is that the word 'bloody' has changed its meaning and is no longer offensive enough. You may have become a 'visitor' or even a 'distinguished European', but turn to the Oxford Dictionary and you will find (or should find, if that publication is really as accurate as it is supposed to be) that 'distinguished European' is a synonym for bloody foreigner.

It has still never occurred to one single Englishman that not everybody would regard it as a step up, as a promotion, to become English; that in the last decade or two quite a few of these bloody foreigners started regarding the English as the laughing stock of Europe and looking down upon the present generation with pity; that, indeed, many of them thank Almighty God for letting them belong to more prosperous and successful nations. No; the pound is still 'sterling', hundred mark-notes are still strange pieces of paper with some Teutonic nonsense printed on them. And if Britannia does not rule the waves, very well, that is only and exclusively because the waves and the world do not deserve it any more.

Old and New

UNDERSTATEMENT is still in the air. It is not just a speciality of the English sense of humour; it is a way of life. When gales uproot trees and sweep away roofs of houses, you should remark that it is 'a bit blowy'. I have just been listening to a man who got lost in a forest abroad for a week and was scrutinised by hungry wolves, smacking their lips. Was he terrified? – asked the television interviewer, obviously a man of Italian origin. The man replied that on the seventh day, when there were no rescuers in sight and the sixth hungry wolf joined the pack, he 'got a bit worried'. Yesterday, a man in charge of a home where six hundred old people lived, which was found to be a fire risk where all the inhabitants might burn to death, admitted: 'I may have a problem.' (Mind you: *he* may have a problem. What about the six hundred? Their's not to make reply, Their's not to reason why, Their's but to burn and die.)

*　　*　　*

Britain is still a class-ridden society. As soon as a man opens his mouth, we can tell in what sort of school he missed his education. Aliens have a tremendous advantage here: they may be beyond the pale; but they are beyond class too.

But the class system has changed. Britain has a working class which does not work; a ruling class which does not rule; and a middle class which is not in the middle but is sliding fast to the bottom.

*   *   *

Before the war you could place a man by his clothes. The rich – particularly at weekends – went around in rags; the working class wore cloth caps; prostitutes wore foxes round their necks and smoked cigarettes in the street; wives of rich brewers wore mink coats and wives of dustmen were dressed as today only Eliza Doolittle is in revivals of *My Fair Lady*. Today mink has become vulgar and the Marks and Spencer era has abolished class differences in dress. There are tricks, of course, and there is Dior, of course, but by simply looking at a woman you can no longer tell whether her husband is a struggling property developer or a rich dustman.

Not long ago my blue raincoat was taken away in the Garrick Club by mistake by one of our noble lords – keys in the pocket and all – and I was left with the other man's blue raincoat – keys in the pocket and all. The noble lord wrote me a letter of apology: 'My only excuse is that a Marks and Spencer raincoat resembles a John Collier raincoat to such an extent. . . .'

*   *   *

Before the war people came here to settle only when they were driven to do so: refugees and immigrants. (In

The cloth-cap image

those days immigrants could be white. But we were white Negroes, really. Today a Negro, as a rule, is black, except that no black man may be called a Negro.) No one settled in this country who was not forced to. Today, fellow-aliens from happy and prosperous countries flock here: Germans, Americans, Swedes, Arabs and many others. The British are poor – slightly beggarly, even – but well-mannered, good-humoured, tolerant and civilised. Their elegant decadence is the magnet that draws people here. The English, on the other hand, leave in large numbers. Their exodus is called the brain drain and includes a fair number of the completely brainless, too. The emigrés are old-fashioned Imperialists who want cash and security. Similar exchanges of population occurred after the war in the Sudeten regions of Czechoslovakia or the former German regions of today's Poland, for example – but those exchanges were enforced, these are voluntary. England will soon be full of completely anglicised immigrants from California, Frankfurt, Port of Spain and Jeddah while other lands will be full of frustrated and morose Britons. Mr Enoch Powell is barking up the wrong tree. If he wants to live among white Englishmen, all he has to do is move to Kuwait.

Language

In my early days there were stories about funny refugees murdering the English language. A refugee woman goes to the greengrocer to buy red oranges (I mean red inside), very popular on the Continent and called blood oranges.

'I want two pounds of bloody oranges.'

'What sort of oranges, dear?' asked the greengrocer, a little puzzled.

'Bloody oranges.'

'Hm . . .' He thinks. 'I see. For juice?'

'Yes, we are.'

Another story dates from two years later. By that time the paterfamilias – the orange-buying lady's husband – has become terribly, terribly English. He meets an old friend in Regents Park, and instead of talking to him in good German, softly, he greets him in English, loudly.

'Hallo, Weinstock. . . . Lovely day, isn't it? Spring in the air.'

'Why should I?'

And on one occasion I received a written message from an Austrian gentleman, that he wanted to speak to me urgently 'in the nearest convenience'.

Those days are over. Not only former refugees but the

whole world has learnt to speak proper English. Pronunciation is another matter; the refugee may still be the man who has lost everything except his accent. On the other hand, Central European has become one of the legitimate accents of English. Or the trouble with the foreign student may be that his English is too good, too precise, too correct. 'He speaks English too well, he must be a bloody foreigner,' is a frequent comment. And a just one, too, because while the rest of the world is busy learning English, the English themselves are busy forgetting their beautiful mother-tongue. If you want to sound a proper Englishman use no more than eight hundred words and, preferably, about half of them incorrectly. Most Englishmen will tell you that 'English has no grammar', which is just another way of saying that *they* have no grammar. Not long ago I kept seeing Post Office vans with the attractive slogan: 'Everyone should have a phone of their own.' In a letter to the *Guardian* I remarked: 'But I think nearly everyone do already.' A number of correspondents wrote in to tell me off as a pedant and a prig, remarking that the Post Office had used good 'colloquial' English.

Before the war a spade used to be a spade – often brutally so. I remember an institution named *Hospital for Incurable Diseases*. How gentle, how tactful, I thought and tried to imagine the feelings of the patient driven through the gates. But by today a dustman has become a refuse collector, a policeman a law enforcement officer, the pilot of a plane a captain, a man who sells second-hand socks from a market stall a business executive and a dog a home-protection officer.

If you want to sound truly English, you must learn to

speak the language really badly. It will not be difficult, there are many language schools where they teach you exactly that. (If you are unlucky you may choose one of the old-fashioned ones and be taught English as it should be, and not as it is, spoken.) Remember that everything is a 'situation' or a 'problem' nowadays. In the old days a man was travelling, today he is in a travel situation. In the past he got married, today he finds himself in a marriage situation. In the past he went bankrupt, today he has a liquidity problem. In the old days he was impotent, today he has a virility problem.

In our economic plight rationing has already begun. This is kept a secret and for the time being only the letter *r* is rationed. The modern Englishman has a certain number of *r*-s at his disposal and no more. He – and that applies even to some radio announcers – uses them foolishly. He will speak of *Indiar-and-Pakistan* and of *Lawr-and-order*, only to find that he used up his *r*-ration, frittered it away, and now he has to save madly where he can. So he will speak of a Labouh M.P. and of the Fah East.

Do we really have a serious *r*-problem? Or are we just in an illiteracy situation?

Food

'On the Continent people have good food; in England they have good table manners,' I wrote in *How to be an Alien*. Since then, food in England has improved, table manners have deteriorated. In those days food was hardly ever discussed, it was taboo, like sex. Today newspapers and magazines all have their good food guides and many so-called experts send you off to eat uneatable meals. Then it was possible for a much-travelled businessman, even a diplomat, to have no idea what an avacado pear was; today any docker may quarrel with his wife: 'What's that Doris, paëlla? Paëlla again? All right, I know I like paëlla but paëlla *every* day – bloody paëlla and nothing else? What about a decent, honest-to-goodness ratatouille for a change?'

There is no denying that the post-war travelling mania has improved British eating habits beyond recognition. Before the war, the French loved eating and were proud of it; the puritanical British loved eating just as much but were ashamed of their passion. After the war, millions of people got acquainted with good food abroad and refused the staple diet of stale boiled cabbage floating in tepid, salt water. You could eat very well in London in the sixties and seventies. Even Michelin published a guide to British restaurants, partly to pay tribute to this improvement, partly to emphasise that in spite of all improvements not one single British establishment deserved three rosettes.

That much-boasted improvement, however, is not quite so universal as we should like to believe. In 1976 the police noticed that a large number of foreign lorry-drivers were committing speeding offences. They were driving their enormous articulated lorries as if they were racing cars or as if they were being pursued. Investigation established that they were, in fact, pursued: by English food. They were doing their level best – risking their licences and even their lives – to get away from English meals. They wanted to deliver their goods and return to the Continent on the same day. As they had to eat *something* while in Britain, most of them – according to the UICR, the Union Internationale des Chauffeurs Routiers – brought decent continental sandwiches with them.

There is another remarkable development. In those early days one could not find one single English restaurant on the Continent and very few in London. Soho was full of Italian, Greek, Chinese, Spanish and Hungarian restaurants. Yugoslav and Portuguese places came later, to be joined before long by beefburger and Kentucky fried chicken establishments, Wimpy bars and other glories of American civilisation; but proper English restaurants were few and far between even in London. Today, almost everything that is bad in the English kitchen is becoming popular on the Continent while everything that is good is going out of fashion even in Britain.

Take the English breakfast, for example, the true glory of English culinary art which puts the pale and insipid *café complet* to shame. Is it gaining ground in Oslo or Luxembourg? On the contrary – and it has almost completely disappeared from English homes and is fast disappearing even from English hotels. You can make your own breakfast in some hotels from instant coffee or tea supplied in little bags, or you may be served scrambled eggs made of top-quality plastic mixed with outstandingly tasty cotton wool.

But other things English are gaining ground. Fish and chip shops (this is an exception to the rule: fish and chips is one of the glories of Britain) are being opened all over Europe and British cod is being wrapped in the *Daily Mirror* – after all, you cannot wrap up fish and chips in the *Dagens Nyheter* and still less in the *Frankfurter Allgemeine Zeitung*. So far so good. Fish and chip shops are great institutions, but the true horrors and monstrosities of the English kitchen are becoming even more popular.

English grocer-shops are being opened in Brussels and other places where true Britons congregate in large numbers. They sell canned steak and kidney pud, English sausages, porridge, cans of oxtail and mulligatawny soups, baked beans, tomato ketchup and other outrages on the human palate. You might have thought that the British leave this country in order to get away from all this. Not at all. They queue up for them all over Europe. I am happy to report that these imports have not made any impact yet on the Continentals. As soon as the French start queuing up for baked beans, I shall commit harakiri, simply by leaning slowly on my

'Watch it, mate, I ain't eatin' my chips out o' some bloody
foreign paper.'

favourite carving knife. Yes: the day the French start eating canned steak and kidney pie with a little tomato ketchup on top will mark the end of a great civilisation, the end of European supremacy and the suicide of a Continent.

*   *   *

And a final warning to continental visitors. Many have come to grief, not knowing an important British custom.

At dinner parties – on the Continent as well as in Britain – you will be offered a second helping. On the Continent – particularly in Austria but also in other Central European lands – you say 'No thank you' upon which the hostess will shriek, moan, sob and beseech you to eat a little more. She will accuse you of not liking her food, of spoiling her evening, of making her unhappy, of being unappreciative and ungrateful, a bad guest and a bad man. So you protest your appreciation, assure her that the food is magnificent, one of the memorable meals of your life, take a lot more of everything, force it down, get indigestion, and speed on to an early demise.

All Continentals, brought up in Mönchengladbach, Attnang-Pucheim, Hódmezövásárhely or Subotica, start off in Britain, too, with an innocent 'No thank you' as their mothers taught them. And that is the end of the affair. To their horror, the hostess does not fall on her knees and does not threaten suicide if her guest does not make a pig of himself. With rueful eyes the poor guest sees the dishes disappear, and the subject is closed.

So when offered a second helping, grab it. Or simply

nod. No one will think the worse of you. And no one will regard you as a gentleman for not taking a second helping. No one will regard you as a gentleman whatever you may do – so you might as well take that second helping.

Drinks

DRINKS have gone in or out of fashion, like clothes. When I first came here, gin and lime was the most popular drink. Ask for a gin and lime today and people will look at you as if thinking you must have fought with the Duke of Wellington's army. Then came the pink gin era. Apart from a few fossils, who drinks pink gin today? Whisky, of course, has remained a favourite and vodka has become popular. (Justly so. Vodka today is 2.7 per cent stronger than in Czarist times. Some sceptics doubt that this one single achievement of the Soviet State justifies sixty years of upheaval, misery, Stalin, purges and the Gulag Archipelago – where, by the way, not much vodka is consumed by the prisoners.)

During the post-war years the English have learnt a great deal about wine and Britain is now *par excellence*, the land of wine snobbery, beaten only by the United States. The British love sweet wine but all deny this with a vehemence worthy of a better cause because they know (or believe) that drinking sweet wine is non-U. Excellent and expensive dry continental wines are being shipped here, then a little glucose is added to them, in secret. As a French wine expert once remarked to me : 'The English like their wine dry as long as it's sweet.'

British drinking habits are also gaining ground abroad. Whisky, and gin and tonic, have long been favourites among knowledgeable Continentals but nowadays British-style pubs are being opened all over Europe and ale is on draft at many places. Serious Belgians – Flemings and Walloons alike – sip Guinness and nod approval. But if the expansion of British ale is a little surprising, the conquering march – well, the few conquering steps – of British wine is downright flabbergasting.

More and more people maintain that Britain is a vine-growing country. If it could be done under Elizabeth I why not under Elizabeth II? What's wrong with *our* Elizabeth? A friend of mine, in a high and responsible job and otherwise quite normal, keeps reassuring me in all seriousness that his own wine, grown in Fulham, beats any French and German wine hands down. As he produces only twenty-eight bottles per annum of his *Château Parsons Green*, Pouilly Fumé and Niersteiner need not tremble yet. But they'd better watch Fulham. I tried his wine in Chelsea, in a house some five hundred yards from the Fulham border. It was vinegary, indeed undrinkable, and we were all embarrassed – except for him. 'I admit,' he said generously, 'that fine though this wine is, it doesn't travel very well.'

In the mid-sixties I wrote a book on snobbery with the Duke of Bedford. Once, after dinner, I asked him what his own, worst snobbery was.

'What exactly do you mean?' he asked.

'Something you know is snobbish and silly, still you stick to it.'

He did not have to think long: 'I'd rather bite my tongue off than say "cheers".'

'What *do* you say? Skål?'

'Nothing, of course. That's the point. A man likes to drink in peace and does not want attention drawn to himself whenever he lifts his glass to his lips. Just drink and keep silent.'

For a while this rule was followed in U circles. But today people do not want to be U any more. Besides, the one strong measure the Chancellor has taken to solve the economic crisis, is to raise the price of drinks higher and higher. That is supposed to save the country. Like taking in one another's washing. So the drinkers of Britain are really saving us all. Drinking another double whisky is an act of patriotism. Even pink gin. And vodka, too. England expects every man to do his duty.

Shopping

WHEN you, Distinguished Visitor, want to do some shopping in England, you are – as you will find out soon – at the mercy of the shop-assistants, now called sales ladies or sales gentlemen, soon to be called Knights and Dames of the Barter. Shopping here is different from shopping elsewhere.

1. When you enter the shop, as likely as not, the Knights and Dames of the Barter will be engaged in lively and witty conversation with one another. You must wait until they turn their attention to you and that may take quite a while. Under no circumstances are you to interrupt their conversation; you are not to speak until you are spoken to.

2. If there are other people waiting in the shop – be the shop the local butcher's where you intend to buy a quarter of a pound of minced meat or Cartier's, where you mean to spend a quarter of a million on a ring for your girl-friend – you wait for your turn. If the death penalty is ever to be restored in Britain, it will not be for murder – an art the English admire and appreciate as connoisseurs – but for queue-jumping, the most heinous of all crimes.

3. While – say – the butcher serves a lady who is

'You are my heart's delight!'

shopping for five days for her family of fourteen, you must not take advantage of a momentary pause (as you would in France) to butt in and ask if he has any calf's liver – not because you want to be served out of turn, of course, just to find out whether it is worth waiting. You will get no reply. This is not discourtesy: it is simply due to the fact that you do not exist. You may not be aware of this; you may live in the mistaken belief that you do exist, but you do not. Before your turn comes you are less than a dog. A dog would be noticed and urged to leave the shop. But you definitely do not exist before your turn comes, you are a non-person, you are thin air, a nonentity, a body non-incarnate, waiting to be material-ised when the butcher turns his smiling attention to you.

4. Few British people go shopping because they need something, still less because they can afford it. Shopping is a social occasion – an opportunity for a chat, an oppor-tunity to display your charm, to show the world that you are on Christian-name terms with the butcher's second assistant and not just a casual who has dropped in from the street. When your turn comes, the butcher's full attention will be yours. No one exists but you. You are the centre of his universe and that's quite something. You may wax a trifle impatient when – having already waited fifty-seven minutes in the queue, ankle-deep in sawdust – the lady with the large family starts explain-ing to the butcher which of her children loves liver and which prefers kidney, or when she enquires if the butcher's younger daughter has already had her second baby. You should suppress this impatience. When your turn comes, the butcher will be yours and only yours. *You* can then discuss with him last night's rain, your

digestion, your children's progress in arithmetic, the topless lady's photo in today's *Sun* (but not politics or indeed anything that a reasonably intelligent adult would like to discuss with his favourite butcher). In France they would interrupt you with some rude remark; in Italy they would howl and burst out in ribald laughter; in Greece they would set fire to the shop. But you are in England, among tolerant and understanding Britons who are waiting patiently not so much for their meat as for their turn to chat with the butcher.

5. On entering or leaving the shop you do not greet the shopkeeper. Your first words should be: 'Have you got . . .' or 'May I have . . .' your last: 'Thank you'. In between, as explained, you may discuss any subject from the shopkeeper's grandchildren to Arsenal's chances against Liverpool, but never say 'Goodbye' or 'Hallo', or 'Cheerio', or 'Grüss Gott' or 'Ciao'.

Sex

I HAVE never been so much abused for anything I have written as for the shortest chapter I have ever produced in my life, a chapter on the sex-life of the English. People kept pointing out to me that the English multiply somehow and survive as a nation. This, surprisingly, is true.

Nowadays they also point out that London is – or was, for a time – the sex capital of the world. Let them believe it, it makes them happy.

The sex-life of the English is in strange contradiction with their placid temperament. In everything else (e.g. queueing, driving) they are reserved, tolerant and disciplined; in their sex life they tend to be violent and crude. A surprisingly large number of Englishmen like to be flogged by ladies wearing black stockings and nothing else; they believe that those ubiquitous places where women strip and show themselves stark naked to an audience, for a modest fee, are evidence of virility; they think that the high circulation of porn magazines is a sign of high sexuality and not of high neurosis. They fail to see why sweating, topless waitresses should put you off food *and* sex at one and the same time.

They also fail to see that a beautiful woman's knee in

'*Again, again, my enchantress!*'

elegant stockings is more alluring and exciting than the sight of a naked sexual organ. They are misled by their noble democratic principles which proclaim that justice must not only be done but must be seen to be done. They think that it applies to the female organ, too. It must not only be there; it must be seen to be there.

People have asked me many times – with an ironical glint in their eyes – if I still believed (as I wrote in 1946) that 'Continental people have sex-life; the English have hot-water bottles.' Or do I agree that things have changed and progressed? Yes, I agree, things *have* progressed. Not on the Continent, where people still have sex-lives; but they have progressed here because the English now have electric blankets. It is a pity that electricity so often fails in this country.

The fact remains that England may be a copulating country but it is not an erotic country. Whenever I try to personify sex in England, Lord Longford or Mrs Whitehouse spring to mind. Girls are being taken to bed, to be sure, but they are not courted; they are being made love to but they are not pursued. Women are quite willing to go to bed but they rarely flirt with men. Ladies between the ages of eight and eighty (let's say eighty-five) come back from Italy outraged and complaining bitterly about the crude wolf-whistles. Crude they may be, but they do make middle-aged ladies feel twenty-five years younger, wanted and desired, and these complaints are just disguised boasts. When bishops, retired brigadiers or at least young executives start wolf-whistling in this town of ours, then I may believe that London has become – well, not the sex capital of the world – but a budding sex-village.

Another thing that has changed in the last decades is the position of homosexuals. It is a far cry from the inhuman persecution of Oscar Wilde to public demonstrations that homosexual marriages should be legalised. (I have heard of a grafitto at an American University which claimed: 'Legalise necrophilia!' But this is not a popular movement here, as yet.)

I have only one serious objection against homosexuals. They are the most humourless bunch of people on earth – as homosexuals. As individuals, I am sure, they must be like the rest of us: some endowed with an exquisite sense of humour, others crushing bores. But as a group it is a different story. The persecution of the Jews generated some of the funniest, most self-critical and self-deprecatory yet cleverest jokes on earth; persecution of homosexuals has created jokes only against them, never by them. In fact, today you may tell jokes about Jews, black people, Scots, the Irish, dentists, policemen, dictators, our own politicians and even cats; you may tell drinking jokes, jokes about adultery and shaggy-dog stories. In other words you may joke about anything you choose except homosexuals. That is the one sacred cow, the one taboo. Should you break that taboo, however innocent your joke, any homosexual present will attack you with flashing eyes for being a reactionary fossil, an insensitive twerp and an enemy of progress. I wouldn't even mind that. They are humourless – so what? That is their business. But why on earth don't they call themselves gloomy, lugubrious, dejected, glum, mopish, sullen or grim? Why *gay*, the one thing they are not?

On Cat-Worship

HAVING joked for decades about how the English worship the cat, like the ancient Egyptians only more so, I have fallen for the cat myself. It has become *my* sacred animal.

It all started with a little black cat visiting me. 'I like it here,' she declared, and kept turning up. I thought it would be courteous to call her by a name when talking to her but I had no idea what her name was. I had to call her by the generic name of *Cica*, the Hungarian for *pussy*. (Later, she started spelling her name Tsi-Tsa because she spells everything phonetically.) I felt embarrassed at not being able to offer her anything to eat, just as one feels the need to offer a cup of coffee or a drink even to casual visitors, so I started buying cat-food. I did not know then what I know now; that this is the way of stealing somebody else's cat.

One day I was caught red-handed. In a little supermarket I had a tin of cat-food in my hand when a nice-looking blonde lady came up to me, threw a glance at the object in my hand and asked me somewhat pointedly if I was the gentleman who lived in that little red-brick house round the corner. I admitted I was he. 'My cat keeps visiting you,' she said firmly. 'I know,' I replied.

'I started feeding her not realising that I was not supposed to do so. Too late now. She expects to be fed.' 'That's all right,' said the kind lady. 'We can share her from now on.' She added: 'This would have been a tragedy two years ago. I have a son who just adored that cat. But he is fourteen now and he has reached an age when he is more interested in girls than in cats.' 'That's perfect timing,' I told her, 'because I have reached an age when I'm getting more interested in cats than in girls.'

So we shared Tsi-Tsa. That's how I got hold of half a cat. Friends started guessing which half of her belonged to me. The *Tsi* or the *Tsa*? There were some ribald suggestions that it was the *Tsa*. Then difficulties arose in her original home: a new tenant on the ground floor kept locking the door against her and she could not get in and out. She got fed up with that and moved over to me completely.

By this time I was a great admirer of her sovereign views, her incorruptibility, her coolness to human flattery; her aloofness; her arrogance; her playfulness (when *she* wanted to play); her affectionate nature (when *she* needed affection). Some people asked me why I kept a cat. But I did not keep a cat. It never occurred to me to keep a cat. She has chosen me and moved in. You can keep a dog; but it is the cat who keeps people because cats find humans useful domestic animals.

A dog will flatter you but you have to flatter a cat. A dog is an employee; the cat is a free-lance.

I was hurt when some cat-lovers started making derogatory remarks: 'You have only *one* cat?' they asked. Then Ginger turned up. I had to call him Ginger because once again I did not know his name. He claimed to be terribly hungry, so I had to feed him. It turned out eventually that he was no stray, he belonged to a lady next door, he has a good home but a voracious appetite. So he turns up for his breakfast every morning and knocks on my door with his paw when he arrives. As Tsi-Tsa is madly jealous, Ginger is fed in the patio. He is generous and sometimes he arranges breakfast-parties for other cats. Always the same two cats are invited and they eat together in a pleasant and friendly manner. It is all rather formal. I was told by neighbours – who know all the cats in the neighbourhood – that one of the guests is actually Ginger's son, the other his sister-in-law.

Other cats know about these feasts. They keep turning up and looking at me with an air of expectancy. I resist becoming the useful domestic animal of more and more cats but I know I am fighting a losing battle. The stray cats of Fulham have got my name and address.

Some friends believe that I am overdoing things with Tsi-Tsa. Not quite so much as Dezsö Szomory, a brilliant but eccentric and misanthropic Hungarian writer of an earlier generation. He hated human beings but loved and respected his cat. He promised an article for Christmas to a newspaper but failed to deliver it on time. A frantic editor rang him up several times. In the end he put a sheet of paper on his desk but before he could start writing his cat lay down on the paper, as cats are wont to do. To move the cat was out of the question but the article was really urgent by now. So he wrote the article *around the cat*. (The manuscript, I am told, is still preserved in Budapest.)

I have not done that as yet but I see the point. Whenever Tsi-Tsa sits on my chair – at the desk or at the table

'May I introduce my sister-in-law?'

when I want to eat – I move her chair gently and get another chair for myself. I have been late for appointments, failed to go shopping and missed planes because Tsi-Tsa was sitting on my lap. 'But why don't you throw her down?', quite a few astonished people have asked me. But I am equally astonished by such questions. You don't throw a fellow being down. You don't treat her that way just because she happens to be a cat. That would be real racial discrimination: the human race discriminating against the feline race.

On How Not to be Reserved

'THE trouble with the English,' a Cypriot restaurant owner in Islington told me, 'is that they are not reserved enough.'

'You mean that they are much too reserved,' I corrected him.

'That's what I thought for a long time, too. I concentrated all my energies on making them less reserved, less stiff. On making them relaxed; at least on one single occasion; at least in my own restaurant.'

'But you never succeeded,' said I.

'Alas, I did. On New Year's Eve this restaurant was chock full, I had to send clients away. The atmosphere, the ambiance was marvellous. People started talking to one another across the tables, even flirting with one another. At midnight glasses were raised, strange people drank champagne together, they embraced and kissed. They sang Auld Lang Syne in chorus and started dancing – everybody in the restaurant, not a single soul stayed at the tables. I never thought this was possible in this country. I was really happy. And even that was not all. They marched round and round the tables, then it became much too hot and someone had the bright idea of leading the lot of them out and they danced round and round the square. I have never seen a happier and more hilarious crowd even in Nicosia than those dancers in the square.'

'Then what are you complaining about?'

'Only half of them came back.'

On the National Passion

Quite a few people told me that I was mistaken when I made fun of the English queueing habit. It was simply a war-time expediency, it was explained to me, and it would disappear in no time.

It is still with us and will remain with us forever because it corresponds to an inner need, it is a way of self-expression. Other nations need occasional outbursts of madness and violence; the English need occasional excesses of self-discipline. Other nations, under unbearable stress, shout, howl, get into brawls, run amok; the English queue up for a cup of tea.

Demonstrations in other countries are violent affairs, with baton charges and mass arrests. Such things have occurred here, too, in the past. Today, if you are bored, you arrange a demo. It may be about the fraternal visit of some objectionable eastern potentate, or it may just as likely be a protest against the late delivery of the morning mail, or the exclusion of dachshunds from comprehensive education. It may be a demo by coloured citizens because too few of their relatives are allowed in to the country, or a demo by Enoch Powell's supporters against letting in too many. It may be a demo by bread delivery men against the low price of bread or by housewives against the high price of bread. Whether it is a demo by stamp-collectors for more special issues or by pacifists for the abolition of nuclear weapons, it does not matter, the picture will always be the same: a peaceful, smiling crowd marching, carrying boards with slogans and accompanied by a large number of bored policemen. All they will achieve is a gigantic traffic jam but that's better than nothing. Indeed, judging by some demonstrators' looks at frustrated motorists, it must be quite satisfactory.

In shops the English stand in queues; in government offices they sit in queues; in churches they kneel in queues; at sales time, they lie in queues all night in Oxford Street.

I was queueing myself once at the snack-bar of Hurlingham Club. The queue was long. In front of me there was a patient and silent middle-aged English couple and in front of them three crazy foreign women talking to one another in loud voices and with atrocious German accents. They had forgotten to collect their cutlery when joining the queue and they had forgotten to collect their salad from a side-table, so they were rushing backward and forward, cackling 'I am *so* sorry' with what they must have believed to be impeccable English manners. When they broke the sacred order of the queue once again, the taciturn Englishman started losing his temper and was obviously about to say something rather strong, when his wife warned him: 'Don't, Giles, they're not English.'

That settled it. The man calmed down and took no further notice of the three irritating females. As they were not English one could not expect them to behave.

'Ssh – I think she's probably foreign.'

Perhaps one *could* train hedgehogs, chimpanzees or foreigners to queue up in an orderly fashion, but it is not worth the trouble.

Yes, I do see the tormenting need in the English for frequent bouts of self-discipline. So I used to be puzzled by the behaviour of football fans. How did their nauseating vandalism fit my theory? I had to investigate, and my findings are not at all surprising: 97.2 per cent of all supporters of Manchester United are foreigners, mostly Dutch and Albanians. Of the rest, 2.8 per cent are Irish and Czechoslovakian, which leaves just a handful of English supporters. After the defeats of their Club these two or three English people queue up for cigarettes, then for sandwiches, then for beer, and having let off steam in true English fashion, they go home to queue up for their supper. The rest? No, Giles, they are not English.

On Not Complaining

You must never complain. Complaining is very un-English. If you are kept waiting half an hour in a shop by the Knights of the Barter; if a bus conductor or a Labour Exchange official is rude to you; if a waiter brings your food ice-cold – you keep your mouth shut. Sometimes in a shop, in offices or some other public place an offensive or sarcastic remark may be made about you in the third person, but you just don't hear it. The stiff upper lip is the British way. Only the Dutch and the Albanians (with a few odd Irish, Czechoslovaks and suchlike thrown in) will make a row, protest loudly or call for the manager.

Should you be so misguided as to complain, or at least murmur, public opinion will instantly turn against you: 'Who does he think he is?'

The waiter may pour tomato juice down your collar and you exclaim 'Ouch!' Someone will be sure to remark: 'It's difficult to please some people.'

So do not complain. Never complain. Whatever happens, remember the new national slogan: *'It's one of those things.'* When your brand-new toasting machine goes up in flames and toasts you instead of your bread, you nod: 'It's one of those things,' and the matter is closed. Apart from being utterly un-English, un-Scottish and un-Welsh to complain, there is another reason for not opening your mouth. They do not even hear the complaints; their ears are not tuned to them.

A friend of mine, a film writer, was a regular client at a famous and expensive Soho restaurant. At 2 p.m. precisely (and at 9 p.m. at dinner time), the office door opened and an elderly gentleman in morning coat came out (as he had been doing for the last thirty-seven years), went from table to table, bowed slightly and asked: 'Did you enjoy your meal?' For thirty-seven years hundreds of thousands of properly brought up English people replied to him: 'Very much indeed.' The man bowed once again, said 'Thank you very much,' and moved on to the next table.

One day the lunch was so abominable that my friend (Dutch mother, Albanian father, one Irish, one Czechoslovakian grandmother) decided to tell him the naked truth. At 2 o'clock the door opened and the antiquated manager came out as usual. When he reached my friend's table he bowed and asked yet again the question he had asked a million times in thirty-seven years 'Did you enjoy your meal, sir?'

My friend replied: 'Not at all. It was lousy.'

The manager bowed with his customary, obsequious smile: 'Thank you very much, sir.'

And moved on, satisfied.

Bank Holidays

IT is the sign of a poor society that it has too many
holidays. A poor society is often a religious society: it
has given up all hope that the government will improve
its lot so it puts its hope in God. England used to have
five holidays per annum and that was that. Then she
added New Year's Day because of the prevailing 'absenteeism' on that day: nobody worked in any case. Soon
there was talk in some places of making Wednesday
afternoons holidays, too: everyone slipped away to watch
football matches, so nobody worked in any case. Then
England started messing about with substitute, supple-
mentary and compensatory holidays. When Christmas
Day and Boxing Day fell on Saturday and Sunday, the
Government decided that the following Monday was
Christmas Day and Tuesday Boxing Day. (Jesus was not
born on December 25 in any case; and what has modern
Christmas to do with Jesus?) When New Year's Day
fell on a Saturday (as in 1977), Monday January 3 became a holiday, because what will the poor worker gain
from being an absentee, whether official or not, on a day
when he would have been absent anyway? There'd be no
fun in it. In 1976–77 Christmas plus New Year lasted for

two weeks, and this is only the dawn of the shape of things to come.

The world looks at Britain askance. Why don't they work? Why don't they, at least, pretend to work? The world, as usual, does not understand. We, the noble British, have three excellent reasons for acting as we do: because we are 1, realists; 2, moral; and 3, practical.

1. As we are a poor nation we behave like a poor nation. We are neither snobbish (not in that way) nor pretentious – so why act like a rich nation? Other poor nations have a lot of holidays, so we shall have lots and lots of holidays. We shall stop work as often as possible and become poorer still. We must be modest and give the Germans and other industrious blokes the chance of working hard, becoming richer and making the money we want to borrow from them.

2. We are moral. We hate absenteeism and the lies it involves. One way of curing theft is to make it legal. One way of decreasing the number of violent sexual crimes is to permit rape. One way of disposing of the nasty, dishonest habit of absenteeism is to let employees off altogether.

3. The final reason is purely practical and based on sound economic assessment. Whether we work or not makes hardly any difference. So it is only sensible to save electricity, coal, administration, fares and effort.

Celebration of the birth of Christ

Buses

Bus drivers still play the happy games described in *How to be an Alien* (available in all the better bookshops). But the buses have become much more sociable than they used to be.

Nowadays they travel in groups of three. You have to wait forty or fifty minutes for a bus, but then you get three at a time, so you are amply compensated. It always makes me feel happy and prosperous whenever I travel in three buses at one and the same time.

Bus crews, on the other hand, explain that they *must* travel in groups of three, to protect themselves against the wrath and lynching mood of the public. 'But why should the public be so angry?' – I asked. 'Because we always travel in groups of three.'

How to Get Lost in London

MEASURES to confuse the foreigner and drive him to despair have developed greatly in the last thirty years, largely in the shape of new one-way streets and forbidden turnings either to the left or right. There are parts of London which even the native no longer tries to approach by car. But these methods are employed with much ingenuity in other countries as well, so I will confine this chapter to the results of my continuing research into the long-established and specifically English tricks which I first touched on thirty years ago.

1. Some streets, like Walm Lane in Cricklewood or Farm Lane in Fulham, take a ninety-degree turn and thus become their own side streets. If you continue straight along Walm Lane (coming from Shoot Up Hill) you will in fact be in another street; in order to stay in Walm Lane you have to turn sharp left.

2. As a number of cunning foreigners were learning how to find their way about in spite of all the hazards, the authorities stepped in by failing to put up – or perhaps by taking down – many signs which might have given away necessary information. Side streets, as a rule, are still indicated: their names are displayed somewhere near the corner, if not actually on it, and all you need

remember is that the name-plate is likely to be positioned higher up or lower down than you would expect which adds piquancy to the search if you are driving and the traffic is moving fast. But to find the name of a main thoroughfare is often well-nigh impossible. The official explanation is that everybody *knows* the main roads so why waste money on signs? A brilliant argument. Show me, after all, the man from Melton Mowbray, Amsterdam, or Bloomington (Illinois) who doesn't recognise at first sight any section of the Seven Sisters Road.

3. Private citizens help in their modest way by keeping house numbers secret. They refrain from putting numbers on their gates or front doors, they do not light numbers up, and – cleverest of all – they give names to their houses instead of numbers. The Dutch guilder may be temporarily stronger than the pound, but what Dutchman would have the flair to guess that 'Fairy Orchard' is to be found between numbers 117 and 121 on a street seven miles long?

But I have to admit that my chauvinism has been badly shaken by a letter from a girl who lives in a German village. She had read the relevant chapter in my earlier book and she was frankly disdainful of our methods. Her village, she said, beats London hands down – and it does. They have had the brilliant idea of numbering their houses in *chronological order*. The first house to be built is therefore Number 1, although it stands halfway along the main street. The second to be built, which stands at the beginning of the street at the eastern end, is Number 2. Number 3, the third to be built, is on

the opposite side and at the western end, and so on. I
have long been prepared to grant that the Germans are
more methodical and systematic than we are, but to find
that they can beat us in creating muddle – that hurts.
At that I have to cry: Halt! Britannia, awake! Decadence *can* go too far.

How to Panic Quietly

FOREIGN newspapers and magazines never stop sending correspondents here to investigate the 'English disease', to analyse our decline and our despair and panic as we cower in the economic gutter. They arrive here to find no panic, no despair. With their logical minds they know that they ought to find them; but they don't. When they discuss the matter with the British, they expect some defence of this lackadaisical attitude, or excuses for certain failures. But what the British say is this: 'Yes, I quite agree, aren't we in an awful mess?' 'Oh, we are hopeless,' they say and order another double whisky. Try to discuss the pound tactfully, and they reply jovially, almost proudly: 'Yes, I wonder how anything can sink so low,' and they ring up their travel agent to book a skiing holiday in Switzerland. The foreign observer expects the British nation to sink into deep despondency whenever the pound falls two cents and be overjoyed when it gains half a cent. But most Britons have no idea – except on the days of greatest crisis – whether the pound has risen or fallen, and the nation is as calm as it was in 1940 when Hitler was about to cross the Channel but didn't.

One day you may confront one of these foreign journalists, so I should like to draw attention to a few of their stock questions and offer you the proper, British answers.

Q. Why don't the British panic?

A. They do, but very quietly. It is impossible for the naked eye to tell their panic from their ecstasy.

Q. Why don't they work harder?

A. They just don't like hard work. The Germans have a reputation for hard work, so they like to keep it up. The British find it boring. Then, apart from a tiny and despicable minority, the British dislike the idea of taking part in the rat race. They will give up certain advantages – knowingly and with their eyes open – in order to be able to stick to certain values and a way of life.

Q. But do they stick to their values? *Can* they stick to their values? Nearly all their traditional virtues – patience, tolerance, cool-headedness, wry humour, courtesy – are the product of richness and power. Isn't there a real danger that with riches and power these virtues will disappear?

A. Yes, there is a very real danger.

Q. Then why don't they panic?

A. They do, but very, very quietly.

Q. Are Trade Unions a real danger?

A. You bet.

Q. And what do the British do about it?

A. There were periods in British history – indeed in the history of all nations – when one or another layer of society, or group, or individual, grew much too strong. This could be the king, or parliament, or the barons, or the industrialists, or the feudal aristocracy, or the bankers, or the clergy. Their power had to be broken. In Britain it has always *been* broken. On one occasion a civil war was fought, on another occasion no civil war was fought. The problem of the Trade Unions will be solved, too. Probably without a civil war, which is a pity. A civil war would at least enliven the British scene.

Q. How would they fight a civil war?

A. Very, very quietly.

Q. Isn't there a danger of extremists gaining the upper hand?

A. Hard to tell. Probably not. The British, on the whole, are extreme moderates, passionate pacifists, rabid middle-of-the-roaders. But one cannot be sure.

Q. Isn't, then, a dictatorship or some other form of authoritarian regime a possibility?

A. Unlikely. The British are too used to solving their problems in committees, in open discussions. They are used to no-confidence motions, to letters to the editor, and just to opening their mouths and speaking up. Besides, they would laugh any would-be dictator off the face of Britain. When the Russians chased away the Czar, no democracy followed because they did not chase away Czarist *traditions*. Or take Uganda. We keep saying: 'You can't expect a Westminster-type democracy there, they don't have the tradition.' Similarly, we don't have the authoritarian tradition. Britain completely lacks practice in authoritarianism. They don't know how to be dictators; they don't know how to be slaves; they don't know how to be afraid of authority or the police.

Q. With all these splendid principles and lack of

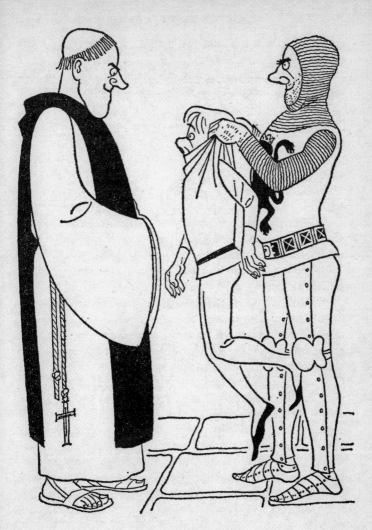

The power of the clergy

authoritarian traditions, isn't there a danger that the country will go to the dogs?

A. The country *is* going to the dogs. But this has always been a country of dog-lovers. So why worry?

On Fiddling Through

You can be as rude about the English as you wish, they positively like it. In any case you cannot be as rude about them as they are about themselves. Years after the First World War – when I was a child in Hungary – people were still laughing about the war communiqués of the Austro-Hungarian High Command. Every rout they had suffered became an 'orderly and planned withdrawal'; giving up whole provinces and running away became 'straightening the lines', and chaos and final collapse was 'strategic reorganisation'. In World War II it took me three years in London to get used to the relish – the positive joy – with which the English reported their defeats, disasters and routs. The greater the disaster, the greater the joy. By the time I got used to the disasters – and started enjoying them myself – it was too late; they had started winning victories and went on to win the war.

It is *praising* the British that creates problems. Praising is 'patronising', 'slapping on the back', and that they find offensive. Tell them 'you are a great nation' and most of them will laugh because no one has spoken of 'great nations' in Europe since the death of de Gaulle. Others will not laugh but will feel offended: who the hell are you to distribute medals? If you want to be polite, call them a 'once great nation' – or better still: 'a once great nation now in decline'. If you want to flatter them, call them lazy, indolent, inefficient, inept and left behind even by Luxemburg and Andorra. Bernard Shaw made a fortune by calling the English stupid and repeating the charge for six decades, because cleverness is a virtue they particularly despise.

*   *   *

When I first came here, the British were obviously unprepared – both militarily and psychologically – for the war which was about to break out. They shrugged their shoulders and reassured jumpy aliens, like myself, that 'we shall muddle through'. *Muddling through* was one of the most popular phrases for years; but I do not think I have heard it even once since the outbreak of the present economic crisis. The British, as I have said, are – alas – getting cleverer. This is the Age of the Fiddle. From middle-middle class downwards everybody must have a fiddle. A fiddle helps; a fiddle solves all the problems; a fiddle is the secret of success or at least of survival. Instead of muddling through, nowadays we are fiddling through. If you come here from abroad, bring your own fiddle and you may get on top. The top cheat – the Fiddler on the Roof – is the hero of the hour.

The Generation Gap

'GREAT craftsmen? Their days are over,' said Mr S., that genius of a patisserie maker, one of the great craftsmen left in this country for whom money is nothing, quality and satisfaction of the customer is everything.

I am no sweet-eater. Old aunts hated me as a child because I never touched the cakes they had made for me with so much care and love. I still would not touch anybody else's chocolate cakes with a barge-pole. But Mr S. is in a class of his own. Perhaps you are not fond of Harold Pinter or Tom Stoppard – excellent playwrights though they are – but still raise your hat to Shakespeare; you may not be impressed by Brasilia, yet you are awestruck by Venice; you may not be fond of pop music but you are haunted by the Ninth Symphony. In other words, Mr S. is the Shakespeare-cum-Beethoven of the Chelsea Bun.

'When I retire or die,' he went on ruefully, 'that will be the end of my craft. Nobody will produce this sort of stuff; and if someone produced it people wouldn't appreciate it. They would buy and enjoy frozen muck at the supermarket. Young people are no good. I have nobody, just nobody, to pass my business and skill on to.'

'I thought you had a son,' I interjected.

Mr S. got angry.

'Yes, I do have a son. He's a good-for-nothing. A dead loss.'

I couldn't ask *which* prison he was in, so I put it more tactfully: 'What is he doing?'

He sighed deeply: 'He's a professor of mathematics at London University.'

Is the Economy
Really on the Mend?

WHEN I was young, I heard this joke in Budapest. A man goes to the rabbi and complains: 'Rabbi, I am in despair. At my wits' end. Life is unbearable. We just cannot stand it any longer. There are nine of us – my wife and myself, her parents and five children – and we all live in one room. What can I do?'

The rabbi tells him kindly: 'Take the goat in.'

The man is incredulous: 'In the *room*?'

'Yes, in the room. Do as you are told. Take the goat in and come back in a week's time.'

A week later the man comes back, half dead: 'Rabbi, we just cannot stand it. All of us are going crazy. The goat is filthy. Loud. Dirty. It stinks. It makes a mess.'

The rabbi told him: 'Go home and let the goat out. And come back in a week's time.'

A radiantly happy man visits the rabbi a week later.

'Life is beautiful, rabbi. Lovely. We all enjoy every minute of life. No goat: only the nine of us.'

The same has happened to the British economy. The bank rate – or minimum lending rate – went up to fifteen per cent. Then down to twelve and a half. Now the

'Rabbi, I am in despair –'

country is rapturously happy and oozing optimism. How wonderful: a lending-rate as low as twelve and a half per cent.

All that has happened is that the goat has been taken out of the British economy.

How to Lose an Empire

To lose an Empire is a bit of a shock. I personally did not like it at all. I am that mildly left-wing liberal who has always preached that we (it became 'we' for me after the war) ought to give it up. But I never expected that Attlee would follow my advice. It is very satisfactory to advocate a noble deed; but it is quite shocking to see responsible people acting on your advice.

The change of atmosphere came very suddenly to the whole world. Before the war Hitler declared that the Sudetenland was his last territorial demand in Europe and all he wanted was the return of the former German colonies. I do not remember one single voice – including African or Asian voices – declaring that the Age of Colonies was over, that all nations and tribes wished to be independent now and that the idea of imperialism was, or should be, dead. People said instead that it was quite reasonable on Herr Hitler's part, we would see what we could do. We hinted that Hitler could have other people's colonies – that would be only fair – but not ours. There were some whispers about the Germans having been harsh and cruel colonisers, not so decent and universally beloved as the British, the French, the Dutch, the Belgians or the Portuguese. But, I repeat, not one single voice told Hitler: 'Colonies? No, you cannot have colonies. As a matter of fact, *no one* can have colonies any more.'

The change on this matter was as thorough as that in people's attitude to female nakedness. But at least between the times when a Victorian lady could not be persuaded to show her ankles and the times when a neo-Elizabethan lady could not be persuaded to cover up her breasts, a whole century passed. But it took only a few short years for nations to cover up their colonies with a blush, hide their dominions, apologise humbly for their former mistake of running a disorderly Empire and living on the earnings of its natives. So-called freedom and independence was granted to all and sundry whether they wanted it or not.

No doubt it is the speed with which it happened that has made losing an Empire a bit of a shock. It is like an individual losing a limb. You can't help getting used to your left foot and you do miss it when you have to part with it. But people react to such a disaster in diverse ways. Some people become bitter and full of hatred and blame others, starting with God, for their misfortune. Others, who have lost a hand, are determined to show that they can become virtuoso piano-players (like Ravel's famous friend) or become football players without legs (like a young and admirably brave little boy I know). Others despair and come to the conclusion that life is not worth living any more. Others look at their tragedy wisely and realise that the dreadful loss is also – like all losses – a gain: you can discover certain aspects, beauties and values in life which would have remained undiscovered but for your misfortune. If you are wise enough

'How dare you, sir!'

you will accept your limitations and turn to new fields in search of new satisfactions. A legless man may be wiser, more intelligent, better educated, more widely read, a better chess player and a more knowledgeable stamp-collector than a man with two legs; but he will not be able to run faster.

If you want to become a modern Englishman you must make up your mind which of the main groups you wish to join.

1. *The Colditz Group.* This group holds that Empire or no Empire, we are still top nation. We licked those bloody Nazis single handed (except that we did not). Never mind that the pound is slipping, it is Colditz that counts. The German economy may be powerful and we may be beggars or at least borrowers (what's the difference?) but so what? During the war (which ended over thirty years ago, about the length of time that passed between Napoleon and the Crimean War, another era in history), well, during the war the brilliant British outwitted those dull Germans. The Germans were brutal, coarse, cruel and dimwitted; the British noble, heroic, indomitable, and gallant. If you doubt this, read any trashy novel or watch even trashier films on television. You can see two a day. It was our finest hour. We – the Colditz Group – want to live that finest hour forever. Yes we want to escape from something – as everybody in Colditz was always escaping.

2. *The Palmerston Group.* Or you may maintain – as millions do – that absolutely nothing has, in fact, changed. Queen Victoria is still on the throne, Lord Palmerston is still our Foreign Secretary. Recalcitrant tribal chiefs will be birched and – in the case of grave

unrest – gunboats dispatched. Some members of this group may have noticed that we do not have India any more; but we still have Gibraltar, Hong Kong and the Falkland Islands. World-wide responsibilities.

Palmerstonians look down with a superior but condescendingly benevolent smile on all other nations. Foreigners are still funny. The Germans have a silly language, whoever heard of putting the predicate always at the end of the sentence? The Americans are even more laughable – they speak English with an American accent, not in our distinguished Cockney or Geordie. The Chinese are Chinks, the Japanese Japs, the Germans are Krauts.

All is well, really the main problem is to keep poor, sick Albert alive because our good Queen Victoria would be very upset if he died.

Only the British are real people, who can be respected, with a few exceptions who are no good at all:

a) the working classes;
b) the lower-middle-classes;
c) business-people, executives and all people in trade;
d) black people;
e) brown people;
f) Jews;
g) foreigners;
h) Londoners and other city-dwellers (if you live in the country); and
 i) country bumpkins (if you live in London or another city).

But as all these amount to only 187 per cent of the population, you can justly be proud of your people.

A member of this group once remarked: 'Running a

vast Empire does – inevitably – create arrogance. The Empire is gone; let's stick to the arrogance. We must keep *something*.'

3. *The Staunch Independents.* Very well, say members of this group, we accept reality. But we do not give up our national pride. Running to the International Monetary Fund or the EEC and others for money is undignified. But we accept no conditions. We shall never – never! – allow foreigners to run our economy. They might cure it. Look what these Germans, Swiss, Swedes etc did to their own economy.

4. *The Little Englander.* England is gone. It has become a country of no importance. It is an off-shore island. A new Jamaica. We know it was wrong to rule two-thirds of the world. Our mistake. We do apologise. We'll never do it again. True, we still have some virtues and assets. We still have some brilliant writers, a magnificent political sense, great courage, tremendous experience, unrivalled skills in some fields but all this is really not our fault. We have not been able to get rid of these virtues quickly enough to fit our new, modest position in the world, but we shall do our best. We shall try to sink lower, difficult though it is, with all our gifts. But we'll try. We won't give up. Sorry for being alive.

5. *The Mikes Group.* Or you can join me. This is what this whole book is about. We will say – and we may be right, or we may be too pessimistic – that nations grow old, just like individuals. They lose their competitive spirit; their ambitions; their virility. In other words, they grow up, become wise, likeable and humane.

If you have to become poor, learn to enjoy your poverty but do not become a showing-off, conceited *nouveau pauvre*; if you become weak, find new strength in your weakness; if you have to decay, decay with elegance and grace. An ageing gentleman cannot be a great tennis champion, a devastating fast bowler or a record-breaking long-distance runner; on the other hand those loud-mouthed, vulgar youths cannot be shrewd, mature and wise old men.

How to Become a Colony

THE British are brave people. They can face anything, except reality. You can tell them that they have lost an Empire and that they are slowly sliding out of the first eleven of countries: that is obvious. But you cannot tell them – so don't – that they are being colonised themselves.

They are being colonised by rival powers. First of all, they seem to have become a colony of Saudi Arabia. Sometimes, looking at certain districts of London, you would think that there can be no more Arabs left in Riyadh. There must be more sheiks in the London casinos than in all of Jeddah. During the hot, long summer of 1976 the country was actually being turned into a desert, with a few oases here and there. We have even got the oil – as befits a country which other countries want to colonise.

The Arab menace, however, is much less serious than it seems. It is true that they buy up half of the country; it is true that they fill the most expensive British nursing homes with patients grand or humble, to such an extent, that in these establishments all notices, menus etc. are printed in Arabic with an English translation (for the staff). But the Arabs, at least, return to Britain a substantial part of the money they make on their oil. Not so much through the nursing homes – although what they rake in is not inconsiderable – as through the gaming tables. This is fair and decent of them. Whenever they raise the price of their oil by ten per cent, they also raise their losses on roulette and *chemin de fer* by the same amount.

The Indians, too, are getting even with the British. Small trade – as a first step – is being taken over by Indians and Pakistanis. In Fulham, where I live, one shop after another has passed into Indian hands: the newsagent's, the grocer's, the greengrocer's, the small post office, the chemist and so on. I am not sure that the Indians were so pleased when we took over their land but I, personally, am delighted by their turning Fulham into an Indian colony, with my television-repairer as its viceroy.

The small, dingy English grocer-shop has become a splendid little supermarket; at the post-office service – and courtesy – have improved beyond recognition; the newsagents – unlike their English predecessors – send me the papers *I have ordered* and they arrive early in the morning. And the Indians keep their shops open at all the hours when you want to shop, not only at the so-called regular hours when you do not or cannot. The new Indian Empire is heartily welcome, by me at least, but alas there are limits to its expansion. At Earl's Court – particularly around Gloucester Road – the Indian Empire reaches Arab territory and this Empire is more staunchly defended than ever our Empire was. No question of granting independence to Gloucester Road.

Even the EEC countries are quick to seize their

Regular hours

chances. I wrote some years ago that the Common Market ought to beware because Britain is not, in fact, joining Europe but is founding a new Empire. I could not have been more wrong. It is our EEC partners who are colonising us. Britain is being invaded. The Ministry of Defence keeps a sinister silence about this new invasion which is much more effective than William's amateurish attempt was in 1066.

Anyone who has eyes, can see what is happening. A large foreign army, broken up into small units, is arriving day after day at Dover and Harwich. They are armed with travellers cheques and foreign currencies with great power of penetration. They bring with them vast shopping bags disguised as motor-cars and shooting brakes. The groups look quite innocent, except that from time to time their eyes roll ferociously and they utter a menacing battle-cry which sounds like: 'Marks and Spencer! Marks and Spencer!'

There is one great difference between the new invasion and that of William: William's army has stayed in England for a thousand years and there is little hope that their descendants will ever leave. The new invaders grab their loot and withdraw almost immediately.

Once upon a time it was the British who invaded strange lands and got hold of foreign treasure in exchange for beads and other worthless bric-à-brac. Now its our turn to be invaded, and the invaders pay with something called pound sterling which they can pick up on their shores for practically nothing. No doubt the moral is: 'Plus ça change. . . .'

On Ceasing to be an Island

I COULD put up with all this. What I cannot bear is our giving up our most sacred heritage. Look what's happening.

I have spent the best years of my life becoming a true Englishman and now the whole country is turning alien, lock, stock and barrel. Britain joining Europe was as if the Pope had turned Anglican or Ghadafi had emigrated to Israel and joined a kibbutz. And even that was not all. Decimal currency has come to stay. Where are the glorious days when every wretched foreign visitor was puzzled, foxed and driven to despair when he had to calculate what he'd have left from seven and six after paying six and eleven? Where are the glorious days of the halfcrown – the half of a non-existent crown? Why is the guinea dead? What is happening to Fahrenheit – that completely senseless measurement of temperature, invented by an East Prussian but so supremely English? As a system, it was rotten, of course, but that's not the point. No bloody foreigner could understand it – not even Herr Fahrenheit, I am sure – and that was the glory of it.

I do not mind Britain becoming decadent but I very much mind Britain ceasing to be an island. And that's what's happening. Not because of the aeroplane; not because of the speed of communications; not because of the invention of nuclear power; not even because of our being colonised by Arabs, Indians and Europeans. The crunch has come with invasion by the decimal point – by kilos, grams, and millimetres, by a logical, easy system of measurement. This is our final humiliation.

I hate being a prophet of doom but I must speak up. When the furlong, the chain, the rod, pole and perch, the peck, the bushel and the gill are gone, Britain as an island will have disappeared and the country will have become a suburb of Brussels.

Envoi

LET us not get hysterical. What does it matter whether we are colonising the Punjab or the Punjab is colonising Fulham? . . . But, you may ask, if that does not matter, what does?

The virtues the English still possess matter. The tolerance, the courtesy, the still fairly decent table manners, the sly good humour, the passion for queueing, the self-deprecation and dislike of flattery, the cool-headedness (even the cold-bloodedness – there's something to be said for not making too much of sex), the gift for double-think which makes it possible to foist airfields and motorways onto other people's doorsteps and refuse to have them on your own. . . . All these virtues, being the result of power and affluence, are as I have said disappearing. But they are disappearing very slowly – slowly enough for me. I am disappearing slowly myself.

Many people are leaving this country: too many strikes, too little public transport, the falling pound and standard of living, the sinking economy, the uncertainty of their children's future: they want no more of all this. Good luck to them.

I, on the other hand, am going to stay even if Britain becomes a desert island with me as her Robinson Crusoe.

Our sly good humour

That, when I come to think of it, would have considerable advantages. The pound sterling would cease to exist so it could fall no lower. If I were alone, Britain would at last be free of class distinctions – the only way, I am sure, that this could happen. Or is it? As a British subject I could always look down on myself as a former bloody foreigner, and as a former middle-class intellectual I could despise the agricultural labourer I would have to become. Even one man can keep up class-warfare if he's really determined.

Even with other people around I like it here. Not always and not everything. But on the whole I like it here very much. Besides, this country accepted me in my hour of need and I am not abandoning her in *her* hour of need (although I have a vague suspicion that I am of not too much help). I have changed my country once and this is, I feel, enough for any man for a lifetime. Let England and me decay together. We are both decaying in good company.

Let me say one more thing in conclusion. When I wrote that other little book, thirty years ago, I admired the English enormously but did not like them very much; today I admire them much less but love them much more.

MORE ABOUT PENGUINS
AND PELICANS

For further information about books available from Penguins please write to Dept EP, Penguin Books Ltd, Harmondsworth, Middlesex UB7 0DA.

In the U.S.A.: For a complete list of books available from Penguins in the United States write to Dept CS, Penguin Books, 625 Madison Avenue, New York, New York 10022.

In Canada: For a complete list of books available from Penguins in Canada write to Penguin Books Canada Ltd, 2801 John Street, Markham, Ontario L3R 1B4.

In Australia: For a complete list of books available from Penguins in Australia write to the Marketing Department, Penguin Books Australia Ltd, P.O. Box 257, Ringwood, Victoria 3134.

In New Zealand: For a complete list of books available from Penguins in New Zealand write to the Marketing Department, Penguin Books (N.Z.) Ltd, P.O. Box 4019, Auckland 10.

THE HUMAN FACTOR
Graham Greene

To the lonely, isolated, neurotic world of the Secret Service Graham Greene brings his brilliance and perception, laying bare a machine that sometimes overlooks the subtle and secret motivations that impel us all.

'Graham Greene's beautiful and disturbing new novel is filled with tenderness, humour, excitement and doubt ... observation of this kind, with every word in its place and place for every word, shows a mastery beyond mellowing age and the fashions of time which we now recognize and enjoy as among the great pleasures of late Greene' – Michael Ratcliffe in *The Times*

BRIDESHEAD REVISITED
Evelyn Waugh

Evelyn Waugh's best-loved novel tells the story of the eccentric but accomplished family of Lord Marchmain, in a social panorama that ranges from Oxford to Venice. And through the bright, delicate beauty of Sebastian Flyte, the heartaches and sufferings of Lady Julia and the disappointments of Charles Ryder, he draws an unforgettable portrait of a doomed aristocracy – at the end of a brilliant, frenetic era.

A FAMILY FORTUNE
Jerome Weidman

Emigrant, hoodlum, philanthropist – and killer, Max Lessing was a millionaire who ruled an Empire of blood and money.

Born from a bootlegger's dream, nurtured in violence, exploited to an awesome fortune, the Lessing Empire was a family business where love and decency withered and died. Behind it was one man whose climb to power was strewn with the lives of those he controlled – and destroyed.

In the tradition of *The Godfather*, this story is as chilling as the world it portrays. You will be appalled by its truth.

'Hypnotic' – *The New York Times Book Review*

MANCHU
Robert Elegant

The big bestseller from the author of *Dynasty* – it'll spellbind and enthrall you to the very last page! The year is 1628, and the fabulous court of the Ming is secretly penetrated by the Jesuits and assaulted by the fierce and terrible Manchu. Here we meet Francis Arrowsmith, an Englishman and exiled Jesuit turned soldier-of-fortune.

Delving back through the shifting sands of time, Robert Elegant recreates the opulence of the Chinese courts, the swift savagery of the wars, the porcelain eroticism of the women and the last embattled days of the doomed Ming dynasty . . .

*Maintenant en Paperback Penguin — le quick method de
Franglais comme parlé par M. Edouard Heath, Valéry
St John-Stevas, etc . . .*

LET'S PARLER FRANGLAIS
Miles Kington

Le Franglais est un doddle! Parlez Franglais, et le monde est
votre oyster. Après 10 secondes, vous serez un expert, Belt Noir
des languages — sans kidding. Ici Miles Kington présente 40
lessons hilarieux en des situations d'everyday. Dans le stately
home, chez le dentiste, eyeball-à-eyeball avec la traffic warden,
dans Soho après dark. Toutes les phrases essentielles sont là, de
'Pas bleeding probablement', et 'Dites-ça aux Marines', à 'C'est
une liberté diabolique' et 'Je suis malade comme un parrot'. So,
prenez un glass de bon plonk, light up une Gauloise et
commencez l'aventure la plus exciting de votre existence!

*Here to delight and appal every new generation — boozy,
bullying Mr Glum, his brainless son Ron and the awful
Eth . . .*

THE GLUMS
Frank Muir and Denis Norden

Yes, the Glums are back — on television and in print in these
immortal radio scripts! As the *Sunday Telegraph* said: 'It was like
being privy after all these years to the first time Beatrice set eyes
on Dante, or Mrs Thatcher on Mr Thatcher. What days of
innocence are conjured up, of Saturday nights at the pics, 4d bus
rides home, Dr Hill Postmaster-General, God's in his heaven and
all's right with the world.'